10 DINOSAURS OF CHRISTMAS

A COUNTING BOOK

BY: HEATHER JONES

1 Christmas dinosaur counting down the days.

2 Christmas dinosaurs stopping by to play.

Stomp! Stomp!
Rawr! Rawr!

3 Christmas dinosaurs waiting in line.

4 Christmas dinosaurs chopping down a pine.

Stomp! Stomp! Rawr! Rawr!

5 Christmas dinosaurs playing in the snow.

6 Christmas dinosaurs with lights that glow.

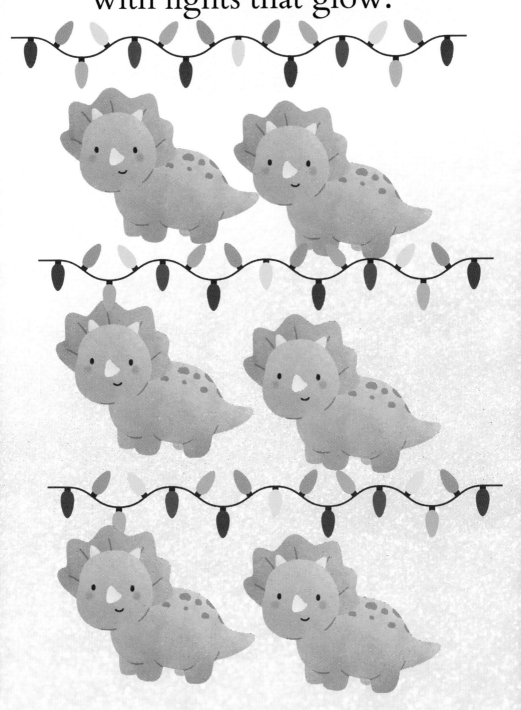

Stomp! Stomp!
Rawr! Rawr!

7 Christmas dinosaurs asleep in their bed.

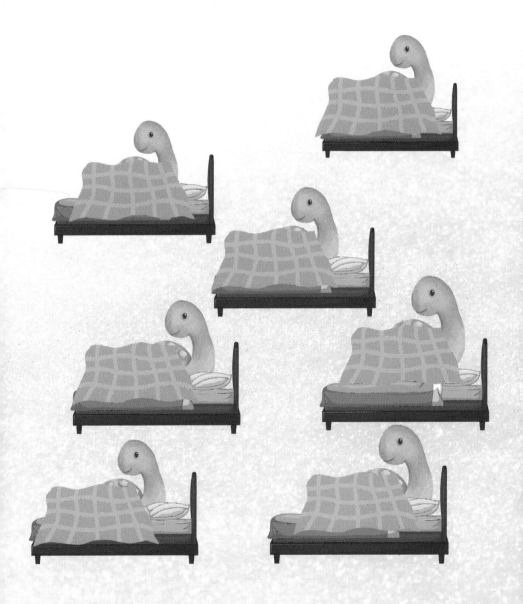

8 Christmas dinosaurs
dressed in red.

Stomp! Stomp!
Rawr! Rawr!

9 Christmas dinosaurs
with a favorite toy.

10 Christmas dinosaurs filled with joy.

Stomp! Stomp!
Rawr! Rawr!

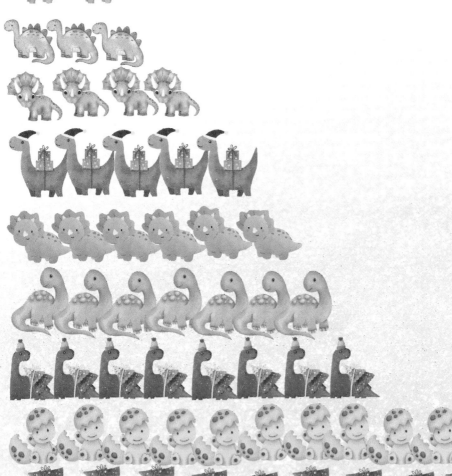

But wait....
there is more...

1

3

4

5

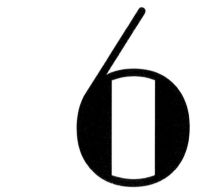

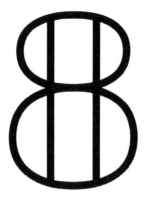

10

Printed in Great Britain
by Amazon

50892090R00016